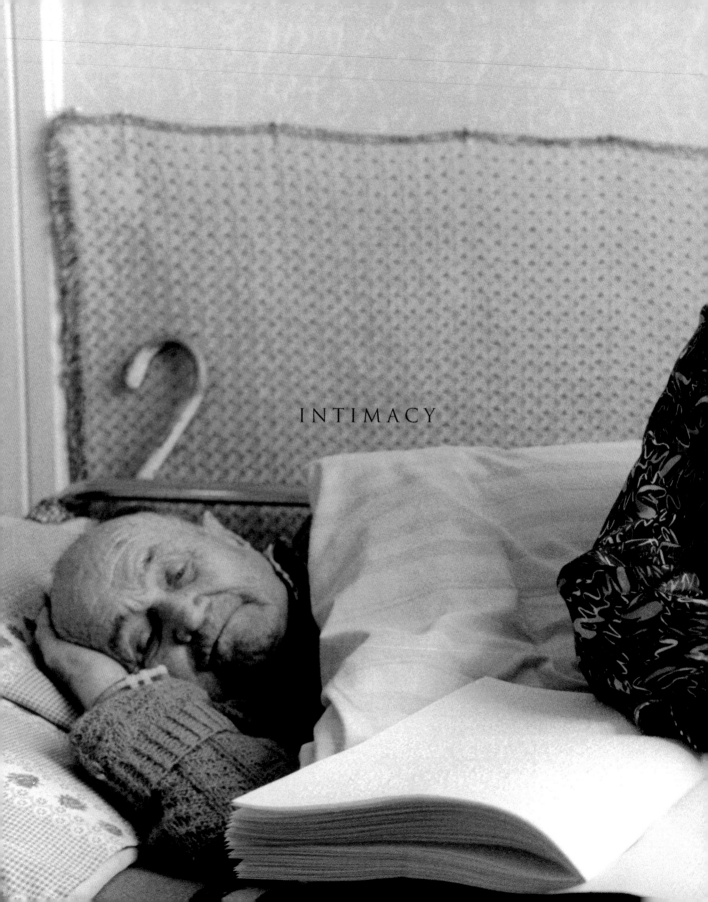

INTIMACY

LAUGHTER

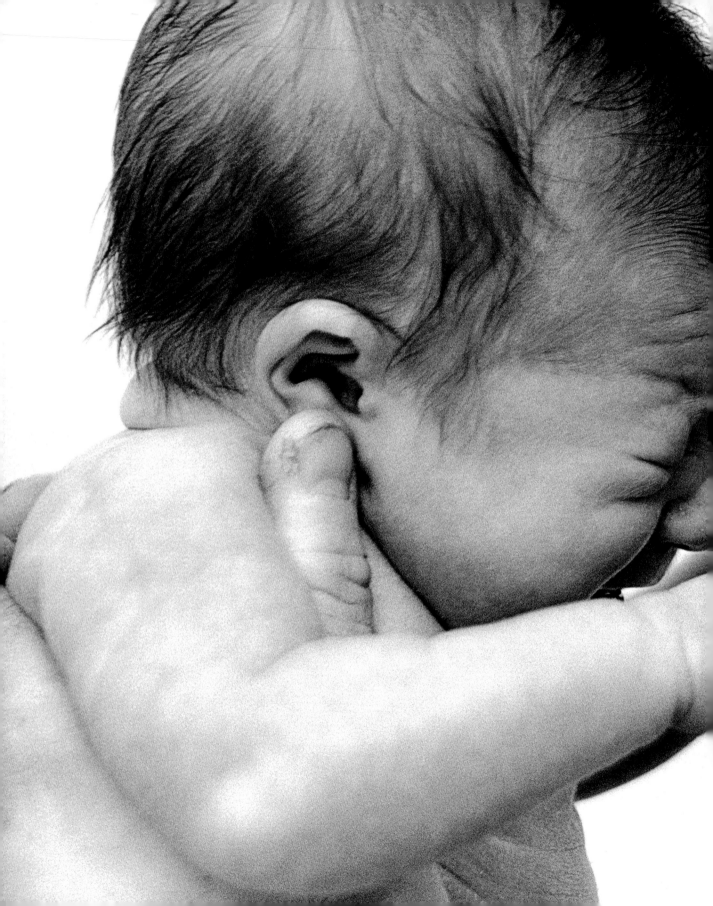

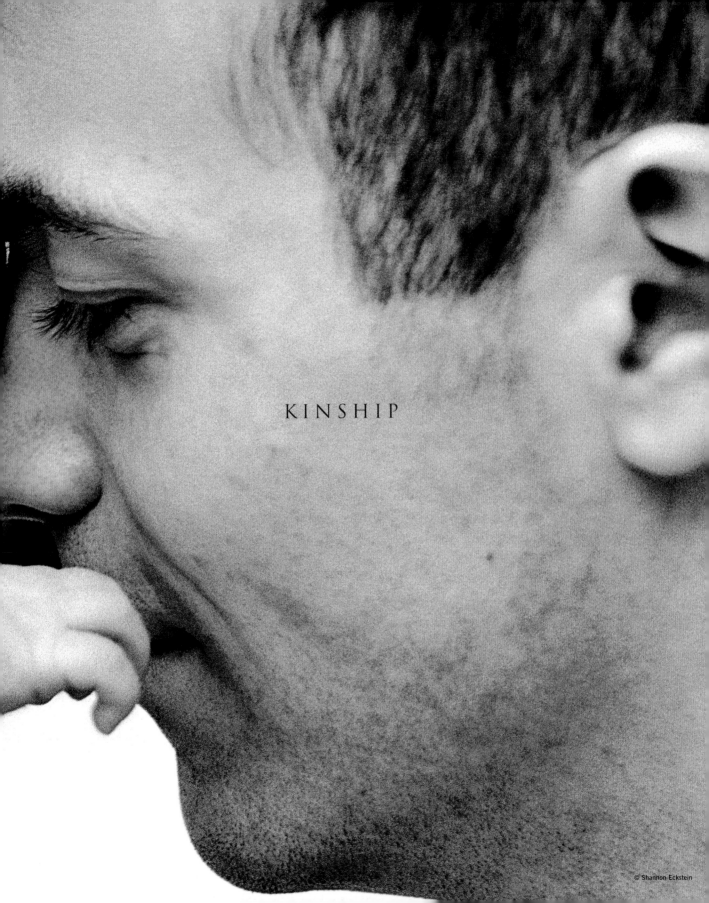

KINSHIP

LOVE

MOMENTS INTIMACY LAUGHTER KINSHIP

headline

M · I · L · K

Only the **soul** that loves is happy.

[GOETHE]

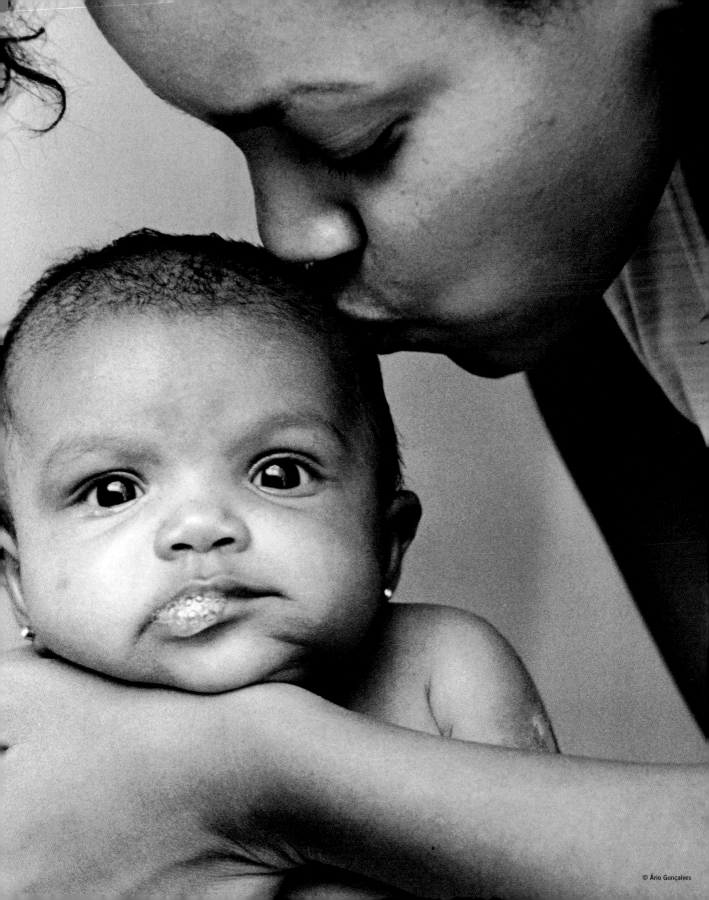

© Ário Gonçalves

Over 40,000 photographs submitted —
some in lovingly stitched cloth packages,
others alongside warm and heartfelt messages
of support and encouragement —
unforgettable images of human life,

from its first fragile moments to its last.

The M.I.L.K. Collection is the result of an epic global search for 300 extraordinary and geographically diverse photographs of family life, friendship and love.

This "epic search" took the form of a photographic competition – probably the biggest, and almost certainly the most ambitious of its kind, ever to be conducted. With a world-record prize pool, and renowned photographer Elliott Erwitt as Chief Judge, the M.I.L.K. competition was conceived to attract the work of leading photographers from as many of the world's countries as possible.

We promoted the competition as "the photographic event of our time" and to substantiate this claim set about the exhaustive task of finding and personally inviting photographers to enter from every one of the world's 192 countries.

Our challenge to the photographers was for them to capture and celebrate the essence of humanity, and our judging criteria called for genuine photographic stories conveying real and spontaneous emotion. Ultimately 17,000 photographers from a staggering total of 164 countries participated, among them a myriad of award winners (including at least four Pulitzer Prize winners), professionals and gifted amateurs from six continents. Over 40,000 photographs were submitted – some in lovingly stitched cloth packages, others alongside warm and heartfelt messages of support and encouragement – unforgettable images of human life, from its first fragile moments to its last.

And so the results of this global search are here for you to enjoy. Our hope – that is, the M.I.L.K. team's hope – is that you will look through this *Love* collection and recognize the people in it. Their moments are our moments. The instants of their lives, captured here, are universal.

M.I.L.K. began as a dream, became an ambitious adventure, and gathered strength as it grew. We see now that it took on a life of its own, ceased to be a project, and became instead a gift.

Along with our dreams, we had high ideals for this collection; we demanded absolute excellence and integrity in submission and selection. Tolstoy, in attempting to define "art", wrote that the feelings art evokes must be comprehensible by the mass of people and not just a few. We agree. These images speak to all of us with clarity, universality and – to use that elusive and neglected word – joy.

We salute the men and women who have shaped this project. We hand over ownership of the dream to all who have been involved, because it is no longer ours. Ours was a wisp of an idea, which has been replaced by a tremendous, inspiring reality.

To the brilliant photographers, to Tim Hely Hutchinson who shared my vision for the project at the outset, to Elliott Erwitt, to my friend and M.I.L.K. Project Director Ruth Hamilton, and our skilled colleagues, to my generous family and other friends who kept faith along the way – and to you, as you begin your personal journey through these pages – profound thanks. All these moments of intimacy, laughter and kinship belong to you.

GEOFF BLACKWELL M.I.L.K.

KIM PHUC

The tragedy of Vietnam, and a photograph, made me a symbol of war. But my real story, like the stories in these pages, is about love. It is the story of the power of an image to change people's hearts.

Many times, when I am out shopping with my family, or waiting at an airport, people come up and ask, "Aren't you the girl in the famous photograph?" They are always curious and friendly. They seem to know me, even though I don't know them. Because they remember an image: that wounded little girl running up the road in Vietnam. Yes, I am the girl from the picture, I tell them, smiling. Then they begin to tell me their own stories. How their lives were affected by that picture. How that picture helped them forgive. How that picture taught them to love. That's when I am proudest of my picture.

My earliest memories are loving ones. The smells of my mother's cooking, the big house I shared with my seven brothers and sisters, Great Uncle's smile, the fruit trees in our yard, my school friends. My name "Phuc" means "happiness", and I was a happy child.

One day everything changed. The war came to our village. My family hid for three days in the only "safe" haven, the nearby pagoda. When some soldiers saw the planes were going to bomb the holy place, they shouted to the children, "Get out. Run for it!" I was so scared and I started running up the road with my cousins. Then I saw four bombs. Suddenly, there was napalm everywhere, and I was caught in the terrible fire. My clothes, my skin, burning. By some miracle, my feet weren't burned, so I could run. I was screaming, "Nong qua! Nong qua!" Too hot, too hot!

That was on 8 June 1972. I was a young girl, nine years old.

Nick Ut, of Associated Press, photographed me on the road that day. Fate brought us together for an instant that was very dramatic, very powerful.

The next day, my picture appeared on the front pages of newspapers around the world, and the world was shocked. They saw an innocent child, who knew nothing of war, caught up in violence. It showed there were no safe places during war. That picture changed the way people looked at the Vietnam War, at all wars.

The photograph won the Pulitzer Prize, but the photographer saved my life. Nick Ut was not just a person doing his job; he was one human being helping another. After he took his picture, he put down his cameras and rushed me to the nearest hospital. That was an act of love.

"What do you think about when you think about love?" my friend asks me. God's love, because God changed my life, I say. Family love, love of the doctors who healed me. Love of freedom and of forgiveness. Mother's love, the love of children – which is so beautiful, so strong, so joyful. Love of a good man. Love of the ocean, of cold weather, because it soothes my skin when I feel pain. Love of apples, of laughter, of prayer. Love of pink. Love of meeting people, especially young people, everywhere. They are our hope, our future. Love of serious things, love of playful things...

In the faces of the parents and grandparents on these pages, I see my own mum and dad, who live with us in Canada. They are grandparents, too. When I showed some of the photographs here to my two-year-old son, he got so excited. "Grandma! Grandpa!" he said, pointing at the pictures, as if he recognized them. Pictured here are lovers and best friends, from many different countries, who share their hearts with us. Some are standing in doorways; others ride the subway, like I sometimes do. You can imagine from their eyes what they are feeling. Like those people who approach me on the street, I can say, "Aren't you the mother in that picture who just gave birth to that beautiful baby? I know you!"

These photographs remind me of sad times and happy times. The look on my daddy's face when he sat for months beside my hospital bed; I couldn't speak, and he was certain I would die. When I was a university student in Cuba, walking along the Malecon at night, holding hands with my new boyfriend. When I gave birth to my two blessings, my sons, Thomas and Stephen. Pictures that tell stories of what it means to trust, to laugh, to say goodbye to friends at train stations. Looking at these photographs stirs my own memories, which makes them so special.

I believe the photographers who took these images must have great compassion as human beings to make such beautiful pictures. You have to love people to take such photographs. Like Nick Ut, I think they would put down their cameras to help people.

On pages 118 and 119, there is a photograph that really moves me. A bald child and his nurse. The child probably has cancer. The nurse kisses him tenderly. She could be my nurse, Hong, who loved me so much. I also had no hair when I was being treated at the Barsky Burns Clinic in Saigon. And because of my burns, I couldn't wear clothes on my upper body. Napalm is jellied gasoline, so cruel. It burns deep under the skin, hotter than boiling water. Every morning, when the nurses put me in the special bath, which made my skin softer so they could cut it off more easily, I would pass out with the pain. I spent months in and out of consciousness.

Then, I see the sweet picture of the nun rubbing an old lady's feet. Touch is the healing power of love. When I was getting better, my family would come every day and bend my fingers for me. So gently, because my left hand was seized up, like a claw, and I couldn't move it at all. Later on, they massaged and pounded my back, to get the blood moving. When I didn't want to do the painful exercises, my mum would say, "Kim, if you don't want to be disabled, you must do them." I loved my mum, and I obeyed her.

At school, I longed to wear short-sleeved shirts like the other girls. Often, I would hold out my two arms and look at them. My right arm was perfect, beautiful; my back and my left arm, so scarred and deformed. Why me? I would ask. I wanted so badly to be "normal". Once, I overheard some girls talking about a boy in our class. He was handsome, but he had a burn on his hand. One girl said she could never have him for a boyfriend, because of his scars. And his scars were so small! Nothing! Not like mine. You cannot imagine how these words hurt me.

I was certain no boy would ever love me or marry me because of my scars.

Sometimes I would sing a Vietnamese folk song to cheer myself up. It tells the story of a little girl who works in the rice fields, in all kinds of weather, sunshine and rain. Like me, she loves nature, but the thing she enjoys most is to bathe in moonlight when the moon is full. If you know how black the sky can be in the countryside in Vietnam, where there are no lights, no electricity, then you know how magical the moon can be. When it appears, it is really beautiful.

I had 17 operations in all. The last operation, in Germany, in 1984, gave me movement in my neck and shoulder. Two years later, I went to Havana, Cuba to attend university. There I met Toan, another Vietnamese student, who became my boyfriend. He taught me how to swim in the ocean, but we had to wait until sundown. Because of my skin, I had to avoid the sun during the day.

Romantic love. Married love. I see these photographs and I smile. Remember, when I was younger, and I thought no man could love me because of my scars? I was so wrong. Toan and I fell in love. In September, 1992, our friends organized a beautiful wedding in Havana.

Our journey to a new life began eight years ago, when we defected to Canada, and it is a story we save for our children. Mummy and Daddy had nothing. We had each other, and we had freedom. So, we had everything.

I am a shy person. For a long time, after starting life in Canada, I wanted to forget that photograph. That picture had followed me everywhere, and I just wanted to live a private life, in my new country, with my family. But it wouldn't let me go. British reporters tracked me down.

Then, a wonderful thing happened. I had a dear friend, Nancy Pocock. "Mother Nancy" was a Quaker, a peace activist, and an amazing person. She died in 1998, shortly after Toan and I had become Canadian citizens. I miss her so much; she had a big impact on my life. At 85, Mother Nancy was still so active, helping people, opening her home to refugees and new immigrants. She showed me that if I couldn't escape that picture, I could work with it – for peace. Finally, I accepted it as a powerful gift. Part of God's plan for my life.

Because of the photograph, I have been asked to play a role in the peace movement. In 1997, I was appointed Goodwill Ambassador for UNESCO, and I am working for a culture of peace.

Because of the photograph, I have travelled all over the world, to many of the countries where these pictures of love were taken: New Zealand, Ireland, Korea, and France. I have met presidents, prime ministers, important business people, famous musicians and wonderful ordinary people.

And I have learned one true thing. The human heart is good. People everywhere want peace. They want to find a way to end wars and raise their families in a peaceful world.

My picture was an accident of history. There happened to be a photographer on that road. But I never forget the millions of innocent victims who did not have a photographer to record their suffering. I especially never forget the children. That's why I have formed a charitable organization, The Kim Foundation, to help child victims of war. It is based in Chicago and Toronto.

"Love your enemies," Jesus said. I have never held hatred in my heart. Never. People ask me, who do I blame for what happened to me? I blame no one. I feel this deeply. I forgive, but I do not forget, in order to prevent the same thing from happening ever again.

A few years ago, I visited the Vietnam Veterans Memorial in Washington, DC. I saw the names of all the people who had died. For what? I asked. Why did they have to suffer? Many veterans spoke with me. A man came out of the crowd and introduced himself. John Plummer told me he had been involved in planning the attack on my village, Trang Bang, the day I was burned. He said he had never forgiven himself and his life had been ruined. He asked me to forgive him, and I did. I think he was a victim, too, just like me.

Another man, Mike, a helicopter door gunner in the war, told me he suffered terrible nightmares. As he talked, he wept. "All these years, I've held that picture in my head," he said. "Now I meet you in person, and you forgive. This is my lucky day." I have many such special moments when I am out speaking with people. These are moments of love.

I believe we are all God's creatures, born with a huge capacity to make peace. The book you hold here demonstrates the love we, the human race, are capable of. With love like this, it should be easy to make peace. We must begin in our own families, then in our workplaces, then in our nations.

The memories I share with you have been stirred by the photographs in this book. When you look at these beautiful pictures, enjoy your own memories of the past. Create your own memories for the future.

Remember how powerful a photograph can be. More powerful than any bombs. As powerful as love.

KIM PHUC [as told to Anne Bayin, Toronto, Canada]

How on earth

are you ever going to explain

in terms of chemistry and physics

so important a biological phenomenon

as first love ?

[ALBERT EINSTEIN]

How do I love thee? Let me count the ways.

[ELIZABETH BARRETT BROWNING]

Let's do it,
let's fall in love.

[COLE PORTER]

31

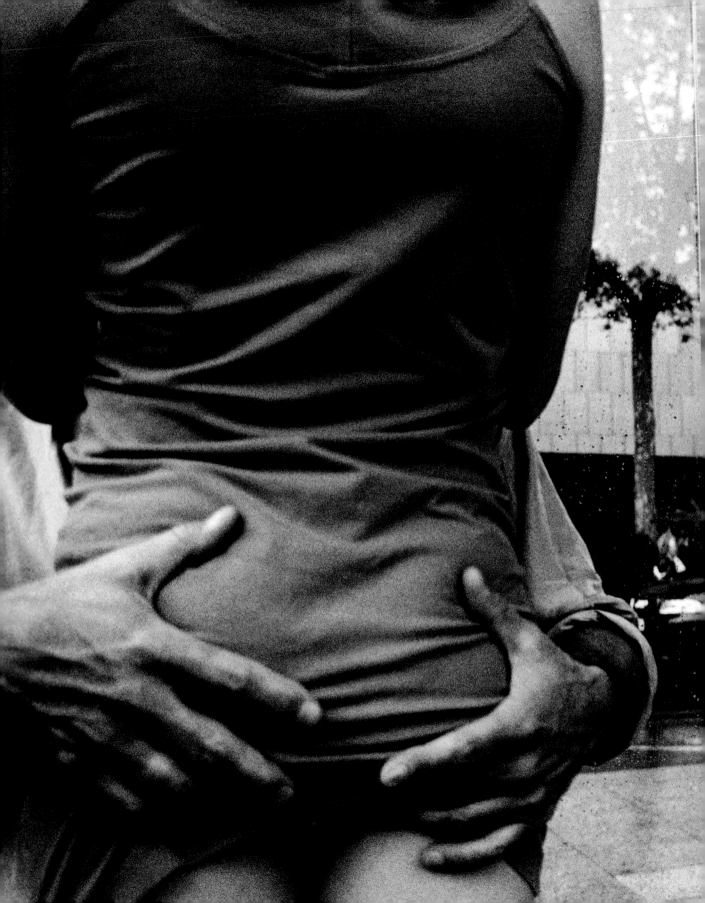

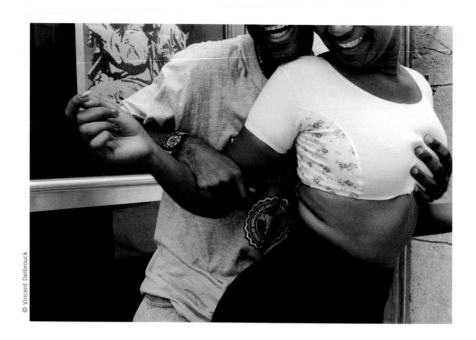

© Melissa Mermin

© Alan Berner

To everything there is a season,
and a time to every purpose
under heaven:

a time to be born...

[ECCLESIASTES 3]

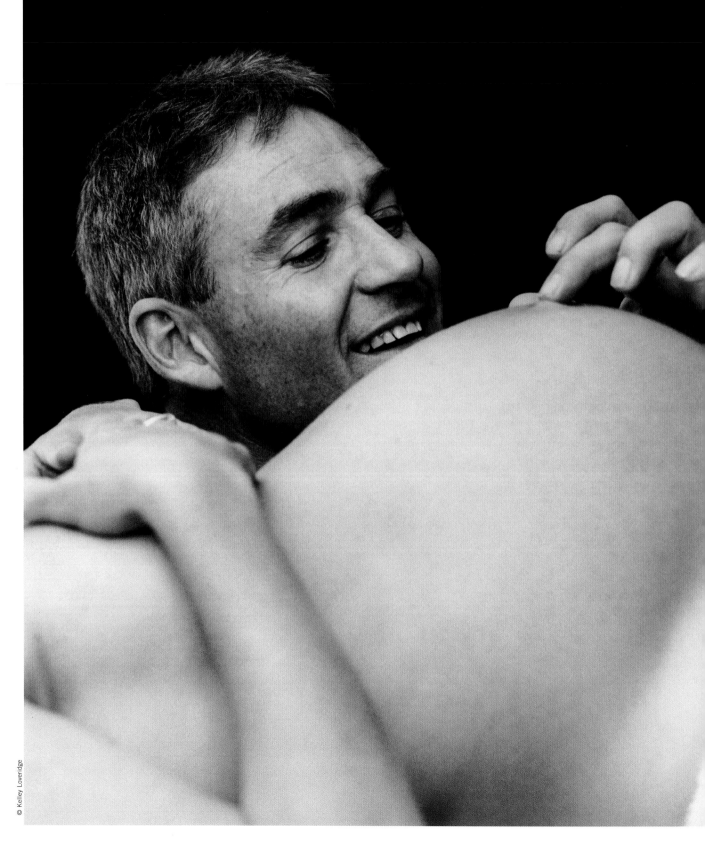

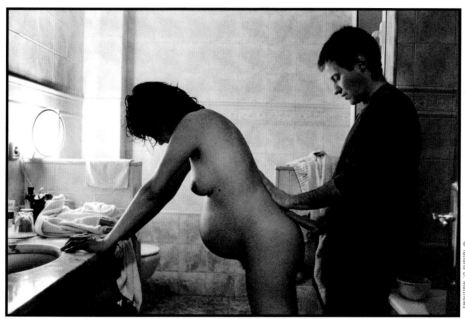

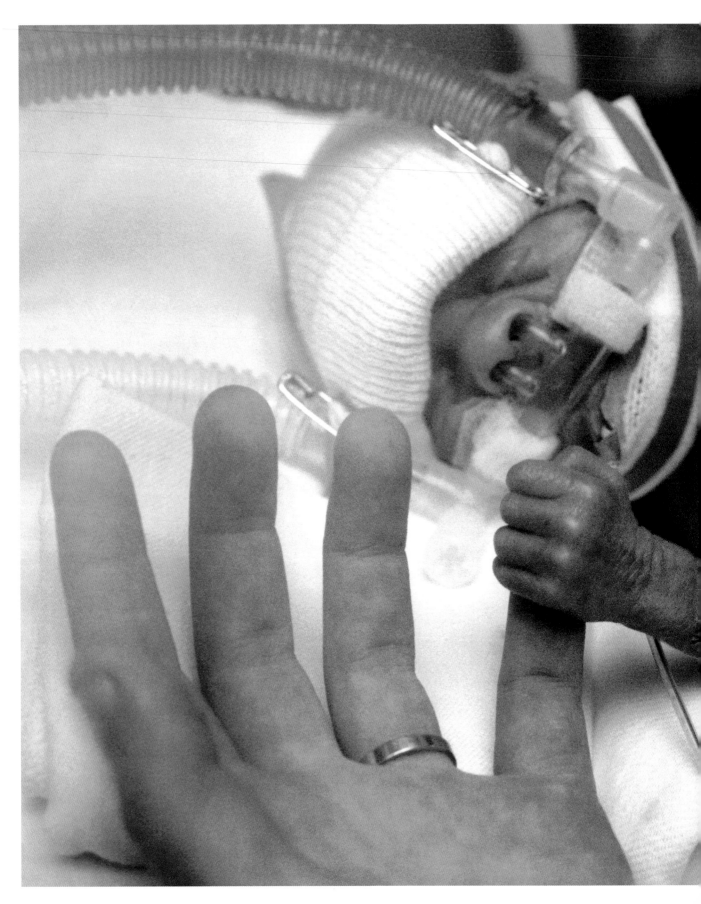

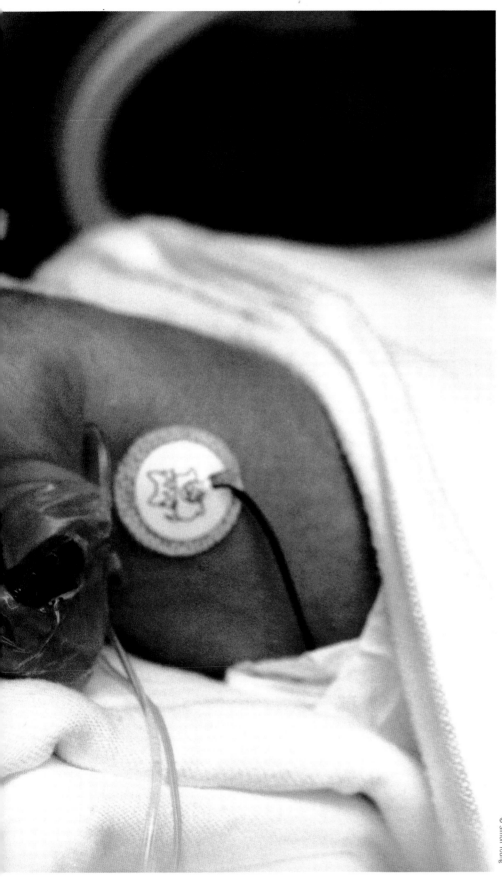

What do you think about when you think about love?

Mother's love,

the love of children –
which is so beautiful,
so strong, so joyful.

[KIM PHUC]

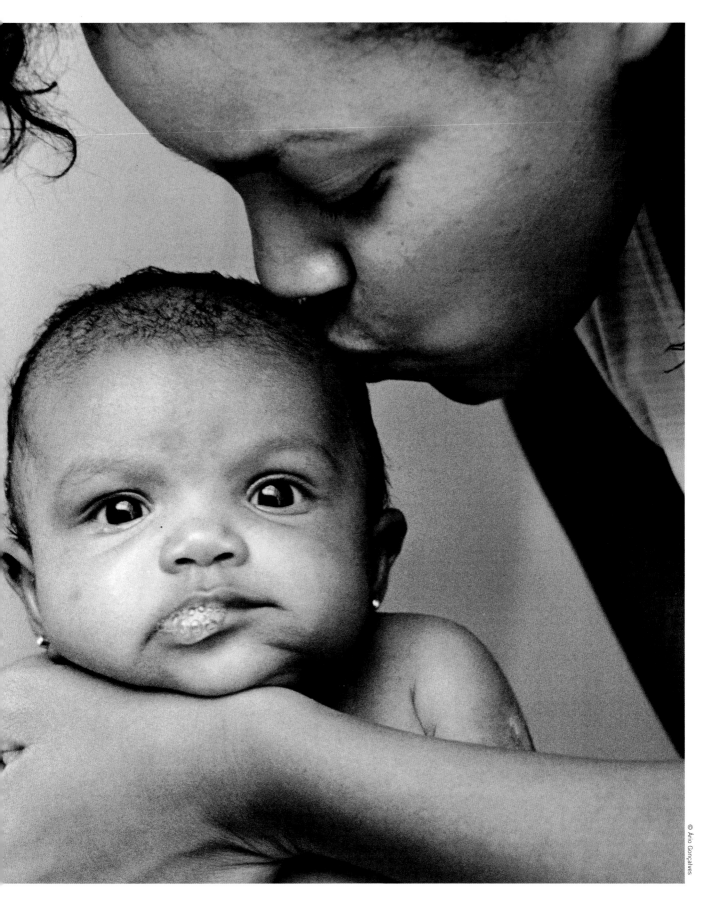

Before you were conceived

I wanted you.

Before you were born

I loved you.

Before you were here an hour

I would die for you.

This is the miracle of life.

[MAUREEN HAWKINS]

I do not love him because he is good, but **because** he is my little child.

[RABINDRANATH TAGORE]

© Shannon Eckstein

© Jeremy Rall

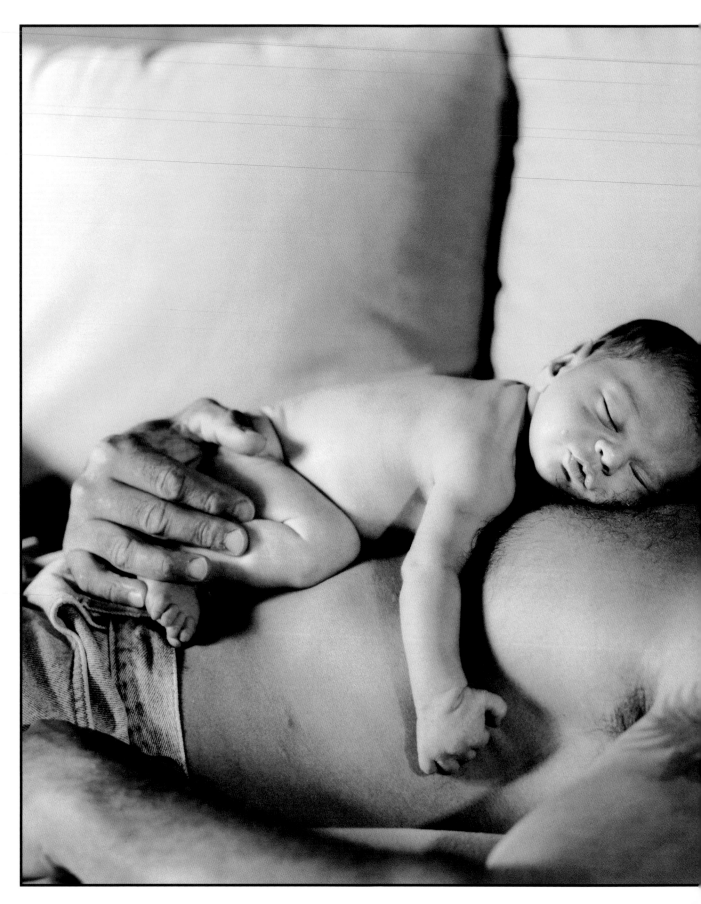

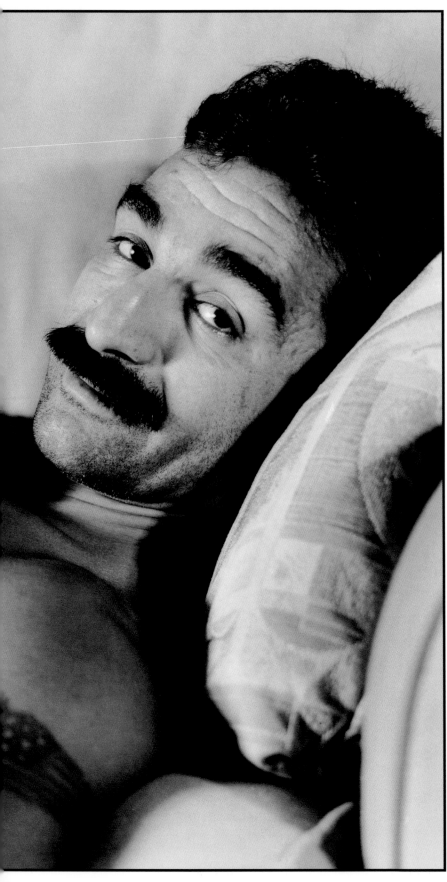

© Linda Heim

© Jarek Kret

The human heart is good. People everywhere want peace.

They want to find a way to end wars and raise their families in a peaceful world.

[KIM PHUC]

Your children are not your children. They are the sons and daughters of
life's longing for itself. [KAHLIL GIBRAN]

Family: a unit composed
not only of children,
but of men, women,
an occasional animal,
and the common cold.

[OGDEN NASH]

There is no greater miracle
than watching a child being born.
There is no mightier conquest
than to teach a six-year-old the magic of reading.
There is no greater force on earth
than the warm breath of a toothless old grandma.

[JAMES MCBRIDE]

© Katharina Brinckmeier

© Devang Prajapati

© Paz Errázuriz

The only cure… is love.

[MOTHER TERESA]

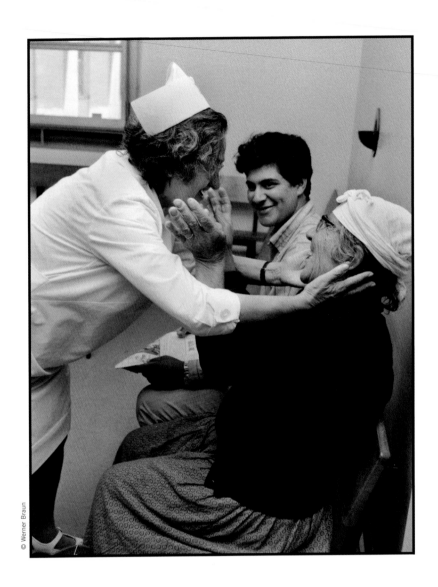

© Werner Braun

Where there is great love there are always miracles.

[WILLA CATHER]

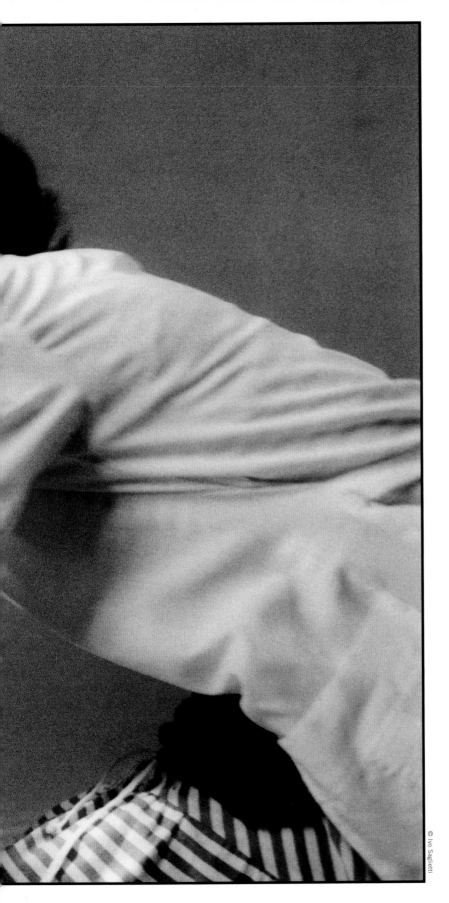

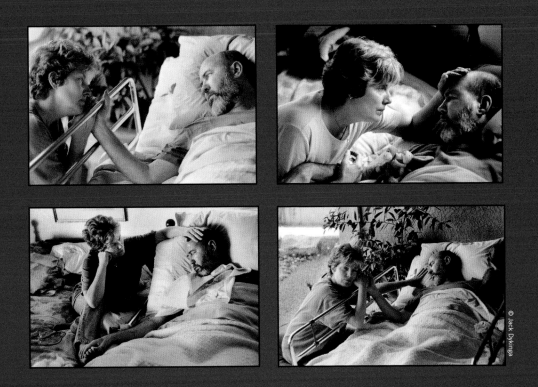

© Jack Dykinga

"My best friend, Tim Caravello, has brain cancer.
His wife, Linda, during the final weeks of home hospice care,
asked me to photograph this intimate time…
a time when volumes are spoken in a single touch and each moment is precious.

This, then, is the final act of undying love."

[JACK DYKINGA]

© Patrick Hamilton

No one worth possessing can be quite possessed.

© Ricardo Ordóñez

Love at **first sight** is easy to understand.

It's when two people have been looking at each other for years that it becomes a miracle.

[SAM LEVENSON]

DUE TO OLD
AGE AND A
NAGGING
WIFE I WILL
CLOSE
MONDAYS

133

There are many in the world who are
dying for a piece of bread,
but there are many more
dying for a little love.

[MOTHER TERESA]

Nothing is more **beautiful** than the love that has

weathered the storms of life.

[JEROME K JEROME]

Remember how powerful a photograph can be.

More powerful than any bombs. As powerful as love.

[KIM PHUC]

Christophe Agou
USA

Christophe Agou was born in France and now lives in New York. He studied music and languages before taking up photography in 1990. He attended the International Center of Photography in New York and since then has concentrated on reportage work. Christophe's images have won numerous awards and appeared in books, newspapers, magazines and within private collections.

© 1999 Christophe Agou

In their own world – on a crowded subway train in New York, USA, a young couple only have eyes for each other.

Leica M6, 35 mm, Agfa Scala/135, Exp. f1.4-1/125

Tommy Agriodimas
USA

Tommy Agriodimas is a senior high school student in Chappaqua, New York. He is a keen amateur photographer and attends all the photography classes at his school.

© 1999 Tommy Agriodimas

A young girl gazes at an attractive passer-by on a sunlit street in Apithia, Greece.

Nikon N90S, 28–200 mm, Kodak Tri-X/135, Exp. N/A

Marcy Appelbaum
USA

Marcy Appelbaum received a photography degree with honors from the Southeast Center for Photographic Studies in Daytona, Florida. She worked as a staff photographer on a variety of newspapers until 1993 when she started her freelance career. Marcy is a winning photographer in the *Communication Arts* juried competition.

© 1988 Marcy Appelbaum

Aaron, 90, and his wife Bertie, 78, photographed at their home in Rego Park, New York.

Nikon FE2, 2/35 mm, Kodak Tri-X/135, Exp. f2-1/30

Marice Cohn Band
USA

Marice Cohn Band is a photography graduate from the Florida International University in Miami, USA. She has been staff photographer at the *Miami Herald* newspaper for over 20 years and has won numerous awards for her images.

© 1999 Marice Cohn Band

Love and friendship illuminate the faces of Sam, 91, and Jeanette, 101, caught on film during a Sabbath service at the Hebrew Home for the Elderly, Miami Beach, Florida, USA.

Nikon N90, 105 mm, Fuji/135, Exp. N/A

Jamshid Bayrami
IRAN

Jamshid Bayrami is a self-taught photographer based in Tehran, Iran. He acted as a war photographer from 1985 to 1988. In 1990, he won first prize in the Third Annual Photography Contest in Iran, as well as a gold medal in the International Professional Photographers Exhibition held in Pakistan. In 1997 he won the Best Photographer Award from *Life* magazine. Jamshid has held personal exhibitions in Iran, France and England, and has also published a six-volume album about Iranian cinema.

© 1996 Jamshid Bayrami

Chahbahar in the Persian Gulf Littoral – Sahel waits anxiously for her fisherman boyfriend to return from sea. When asked about her lover's whereabouts, she covers her face to hide her tears.

Nikon F601, 70–210 mm, Kodak/135, Exp. N/A

Alan Berner
USA

Alan Berner of Seattle, Washington, has degrees in philosophy and photojournalism and currently works as a staff photographer at the *Seattle Times* newspaper. The National Press Photographers Association in the USA has named him the Regional Press Photographer of the Year on four separate occasions. In 1995, Alan was awarded the Nikon/NPPA Documentary Sabbatical grant for his project on the American West.

© 1996 Alan Berner

English Bay beach in Vancouver, Canada – a newly wed couple are in playful mood as they wait for their wedding portrait to be taken.

Leica M4, 2/35 mm, Kodak Tri-X/135, Exp. f5.6-1/125

Robert Billington
AUSTRALIA

Robert Billington, based in Sydney, has been a professional photographer for over 18 years and has won many awards for his pictures of people and landscapes. He has published four books of his documentary photographs. Robert was named Australian Professional Photographer of the Year in 1994 and Australian Editorial Photographer of the Year in 1999.

© 1999 Robert Billington

At the end of the Shark Island swimming race in Sydney, Australia, a one-legged competitor emerges from the surf. His young son hurries over with his artificial limb. This teamwork means his father can run to the finishing line.

Rolleiflex GL2.8, 80 mm, Kodak T-max/120, Exp. f11-1/250

Werner Braun
ISRAEL

Werner Braun was born in Nuremberg in Germany. He emigrated to Palestine in 1946 and soon began a career as a press photographer, often documenting terrorist actions. Werner was the official photographer at the trial of Adolf Eichmann in Jerusalem. He has published over 20 books during the course of his career and, in 1998, the city of Nuremberg held an exhibition of his work to celebrate his 80th birthday.

© 1973 Werner Braun

An affectionate greeting between a nurse and her elderly patient enlivens a hospital waiting room in Jerusalem, Israel.

Hasselblad, 80 mm, Ilford HP4/120, Exp. f5.6-1/60

Katharina Brinckmeier
THE NETHERLANDS

Katharina Brinckmeier was born in Germany and today lives in Haarlem in the Netherlands. She was educated as a painter and a movement therapist and currently works as an artist. Katharina has been interested in photography since 1978 and, following the birth of her daughter, now concentrates particularly on portrait work.

© 1999 Katharina Brinckmeier

The special relationship between two-year-old Mayra and her grandmother Mutti, 92, captured on film in the village of Rautheim in Braunschweig, Germany.

Minolta 7000AF, 2.8/55 mm, Kodak TMY/135, Exp. N/A

Everett Kennedy Brown
JAPAN

Everett Kennedy Brown is a photojournalist based in Japan whose work appears regularly in the Japanese media. His photographic projects have included documentation of the historical botanical gardens of the world and the disappearing rituals of the Japanese archipelago. He has received critical acclaim for his book *Eyes on Japan*, a photographic and literary insight into the lives of international sports figures in Japan.

© 1997 Everett Kennedy Brown

On a journey through the steppes of Inner Mongolia in China, new friends pause to feed their horses and to share a moment of quiet affection.

Nikon F4, 1.4/35 mm, Kodak Tri-X/135, Exp. f5.6-1/60

Romano Cagnoni
ITALY

Romano Cagnoni was born in Italy but moved to London, England, to study with photojournalism expert Simon Guttman. Romano was the first photographer admitted to North Vietnam in 1965 and since then has documented many world events for a range of international magazines. He has won the USA Overseas Press Award and numerous other prizes. Harold Evans, the former editor of the *Sunday Times* in London, mentions Romano among the seven most famous photographers in the world in his book *Pictures on a Page*.

© 1981 Romano Cagnoni

On a beach in Cleethorpes, England, a fairground rocket provides the backdrop for a young couple's playful romp in the sand.

Nikon F2, 180 mm, Kodak/135, Exp. f8-1/250

José Caldas
BRAZIL

José Caldas is based in Rio de Janeiro, Brazil. He has been a professional photographer for over 14 years and specializes in nature photography. José's work has been published in a variety of Brazilian and international magazines, as well as appearing in the *Britannica* and *Encarta* encyclopedias. In 1992, José was awarded the Marc Ferrez IBAC Funarte Prize for his photographic documentation of the lower São Francisco River in Brazil.

© 1997 José Caldas

A married couple stand side by side in their home by the São Francisco River, Brazil. Behind them, their wedding picture is proudly displayed.

Hasselblad, 38 mm, Fujichrome Velvia/120, Exp. f5.6-1/8

Krisadakorn Chaiyaphaka
THAILAND

Krisadakorn Chaiyaphaka is a graduate of the Faculty of Business Administration at Ramkhamhaing University, Thailand. Currently he runs his own business in the construction industry. He is a keen photographer and a member of the Photographic Society of Thailand.

© 1997 Krisadakorn Chaiyaphaka

A portrait of love and contentment in Chiang Rai, Thailand, as a young woman bathes and feeds her baby son.

Nikon F801S, 80–200 mm, Fuji/135, Exp. f4-1/250

Claude Coirault
TAHITI

Claude Coirault was born in Guadeloupe in the French West Indies. He studied maths, physics and languages at a university in Paris before concentrating on his interest in photography. Claude has worked as a photographer in many different countries on a range of subject matter. Currently he is based in Papeete, Tahiti.

© Claude Coirault [date N/A]

Inseparable companions – the closeness and love of a brother and sister caught on camera in the Ivory Coast region of West Africa.

N/A

Ivan Coleman
UK

Ivan Coleman is based in London, England, and became interested in photography while studying at art school. He now works as a professional photographer specializing in the areas of journalism and reportage.

© 1998 Ivan Coleman

London, England – two tourists share a lingering kiss by the water as the sun sets on a busy day of sightseeing.

Canon EOS 1, 200 mm, Kodak Tri-X/135, Exp. f4-1/500

Andrew Danson
CANADA

Andrew Danson is based in Toronto, Canada, and his work has appeared in 50 national and international exhibitions since the 1970s. Andrew's pictures appear in museums, including the National Archives of Canada and the Canadian Museum of Contemporary Photography. He is also a curator and photography lecturer at the Bell Center for Creative Communications in Toronto.

© 1977 Andrew Danson

Two of a kind – the photographer's great-aunts at their home in Canada. Sisters Rose and Florence have lived together since they were both widowed in their 40s.

Hasselblad 500 CM, 80 mm, 120, Exp. N/A

Dennis Darmek
USA

Dennis Darmek graduated from the School of Fine Arts at the University of Wisconsin in Milwaukee, Wisconsin, USA. He has worked in the fields of photography and video, and is currently a production manager at the Instructional Media Center of Marquette University, Milwaukee. Dennis has won numerous awards for his work, including first prize in the 1977 Nikon National Photo Competition, and the Director's Choice Award in the Black Maria Film and Video Festival in 1993 and 1996.

© 1997 Dennis Darmek

A typical summer's day at the Big Kahuna water theme park in Wisconsin Dells, Wisconsin, USA. A couple hold each other close as they wonder whether to take a dip.

Noblex 135, Kodak T-max/135, Exp. N/A

Binode Kumar Das
INDIA

Binode Kumar Das lives in Calcutta, India, where he works in the Department of Sericulture for the Government of West Bengal. He is a keen photographer and a member of the East Calcutta Photographic Association.

© 1999 Binode Kumar Das

After a hard day's work in West Bengal, India, a mother is delighted to return to the company of her children.

Asahi Pentax KM, 50 mm, 135, Exp. f8-1/60

Todd Davis
USA

Todd Davis has been an enthusiastic amateur photographer for the last four years. Based in Ashland, Oregon, he works as a supervisor/educator in a natural food store. Todd is pursuing his interest in photography by serving an apprenticeship with a fine arts photographer.

© 1999 Todd Davis

Bob drives his wife, Peggy, home to Houston, Texas, USA. The couple have been married for 54 years.

Canon Elan IIe, Tamron 20–40 mm, Kodak CN400/135, Exp. N/A

Michael Decher
GERMANY

Michael Decher is based in Erlangen, Germany. He is a qualified speech therapist and a self-taught photographer. He now works as an independent photographer and his images have appeared in numerous newspapers and books. His work has been displayed in exhibitions in Germany, Denmark and Switzerland, and in collections in Europe and the USA.

© 1997 Michael Decher

"Klara and me" – this self-portrait captures a father's face full of tenderness and love as he holds his one-week-old daughter.

Canon F1, 2.8/90 mm, Ilford Delta 400/135, Exp. 1/30

Vincent Delbrouck
BELGIUM

Vincent Delbrouck is a graduate in social communication. Currently he and his wife work as a documentary photography team based in Brussels, Belgium.

© 1997 Vincent Delbrouck

Young lovers clasp each other tight as they dance to the rhythms of Havana, Cuba.

Olympus, 35 mm, Ilford HP5/135, Exp. N/A

Sergey Denisov
KAZAKHSTAN

Sergey Denisov was born in Kazakh, formerly part of the USSR. He studied metallurgy at the Kazakh Polytechnic Institute, but decided instead to pursue a career in photography. He has been a keen photographer for over 30 years and currently works as a freelancer in Almaty, Kazakhstan.

© 1996 Sergey Denisov

Memories are shared at the Day of Victory in Almaty, Kazakhstan. On this annual occasion, war veterans come to the Memorial Park to honour the memory of their loved ones and renew contact with old friends.

Zenit TTL, 80–200 mm, Fuji Super G Plus 200/135, Exp. f8-1/125

Carol Dupree
USA

Carol Dupree lives in Florida, USA, and became interested in photography while at college. After being asked to photograph the birth of her friend's child, she went on to capture other births on film and has now set up her own business, Spontaneous Exposures.

© 1998 Carol Dupree

The moment of birth captured on film in Gainesville, Florida, USA – as baby Wyatt takes his first breath, Taylor gives exhausted mother Sydney a loving kiss.

Nikon 2020, 28–80 mm, Kodak T-max/135, Exp. N/A

Jack Dykinga
USA

Jack Dykinga is a Pulitzer Prize winning photographer who won the award for feature photography while working on the *Chicago Sun Times*. He moved to the city of Tucson in 1976 and since then has devoted his time to landscape photography and environmental issues. The publication of Jack's images in several books has led to the creation of National Parks and preserves in both the USA and Mexico. His latest book concentrates on the Mojave Desert region of the USA.

© 1999 Jack Dykinga

Undying love – a series of pictures of the photographer's best friend, Tim Caravello, in the last weeks of his battle with brain cancer. During the final stages of home hospice care in Tucson, Arizona, USA, Tim's wife Linda asked Jack Dykinga to photograph this intimate and emotional time.

Nikon N90S, 2.8/35 mm and 1.8/70–105 mm, Kodak Tri-X/135, Exp. f2.8-1/30 and f2-1/125

Shannon Eckstein
CANADA

Shannon Eckstein was born in Canada and spent seven years travelling around the world before returning to Vancouver. In 1998 she set up her own company, Silvershadow Photographic Images, which specializes in innovative black and white photography for a wide range of clients.

© 1999 Shannon Eckstein

Rubbing noses in Vancouver, Canada – new father Davy finds the perfect way to bond with his baby daughter, Ciara, only nine days old.

Nikon 90X, 24–120 mm, Agfa 100/135, Exp. f5.6-1/125

Sandra Eleta
PANAMA

Sandra Eleta was born in Panama. She travelled extensively abroad before heading to New York, to study at the International Center of Photography. After graduation, she returned to her home country to pursue her interest and lives today in Panama City.

© 1979 Sandra Eleta

The spirit of the old Latin American phrase "tienes luz en la pupila" – "you have light in your eyes" – is captured in this photograph of Putulungo and Alma, taken in Portobelo, Panama.

Hasselblad 500C, 80 mm, Kodak Tri-X/120, Exp. f5.6

Mark Engledow
USA

Mark Engledow spent 20 years in the radio business before becoming a professional photographer. He concentrates particularly on nature, landscape and wildlife photography, but has also won numerous awards for his journalistic images of people and places. Mark now lives in Fort Myers, Florida, and is a member of the association of Florida Professional Photographers.

© 1977 Mark Engledow

The photographer's daughter – six-year-old Kitty – stretches on tip-toe to give her grandfather, Bert, a kiss in Bloomington, Indiana, USA.

Ricoh KR10, 30–80 mm, Ilford FP4/135, Exp. f5.6-1/500

Lloyd Erlick
CANADA

Lloyd Erlick is a professional photographic portrait artist specializing in black and white images. He is based in Toronto, Canada.

© 1997 Lloyd Erlick

Family portrait in Toronto, Canada – proud mother Caitlin gently holds six-month-old Shai as she reaches out to greet her great-grandmother, Natalie.

Hasselblad ELX, 120 mm, Kodak TMY/120, Exp. f8-1/15

Paz Errázuriz
CHILE

Paz Errázuriz is a self-taught photographer from Santiago, Chile. She studied education at the Catholic University in Santiago and, after graduation, worked as a primary school teacher. After leaving the teaching profession, she became an independent photographer for magazines and Fundacion Andes. She was awarded a Guggenheim Fellowship in 1987, and has had two books published.

© 1992 Paz Errázuriz

A portrait of the loving kindness of the nuns who run this resthome in Santiago, Chile.

Nikon F2, 50 mm, Kodak Tri-X/135, Exp. f8-1/60

Mikhail Evstafiev
RUSSIA

Mikhail Evstafiev was born in Moscow, Russia, and studied international journalism at the Moscow State University. After graduation, he worked as a reporter and then spent two years as a military correspondent in Afghanistan. He became a freelance photographer in 1990 followed by work for Agence France-Presse, and for Reuters in Moscow and London. Mikhail is the author of the book *Two Steps from Heaven* about the Soviet war in Afghanistan.

© 1999 Mikhail Evstafiev

On the streets of Santiago de Cuba, Cuba – a couple's uninhibited display of affection raises a spontaneous smile from their young audience.

Leica M6, 28 mm, Ilford XP2/135, Exp. f5.6-1/125

Barbara Judith Exeter
NEW ZEALAND

Barbara Judith Exeter is an amateur photographer who lives in Napier, New Zealand. Her favourite photographic subjects are the children and grandchildren of the family.

© 1998 Barbara Judith Exeter

A mother's face is a picture of relief after the birth of her first child in Hastings, New Zealand. After 32 hours in labour, Linda is exhausted, but ecstatic, as father Wayne admires baby Braeden, only five minutes old.

Weathermatic 35DL, 3.5/35 mm, Kodak Kroma/135, Exp. N/A

Pepe Franco
USA

Pepe Franco's interest in photography began when he bought his first camera with money he earned as a bricklayer. After studying sociology at college, he decided to follow a career in photography. He has been a professional photojournalist since 1984, working mainly in Spain, but with recent assignments in Mexico and the USA.

© 1992 Pepe Franco

Father-to-be Angel can't help laughing as he tells a joke to his unborn baby. This image of Angel and his partner, Isabel, was captured during a family party in Aguilas, Spain.

Leica M6, 50 mm, Kodak/135, Exp. N/A

Richard Frank
USA

Richard Frank has worked as a freelance photographer for over 25 years. He specializes in photographing people on location for magazines, corporate brochures and advertising. Richard is based in Westport, Connecticut.

© 1972 Richard Frank

Putting your feet up takes on a new meaning in Indiana, USA.

Nikon F, 35 mm, Kodak/135, Exp. N/A

Gary Freeman
UK

Gary Freeman is a photography graduate from Nottingham Trent University in the UK. He has also studied at the NARAFI school in Brussels, Belgium, and the FAMU Academy in Prague, Czech Republic. Currently Gary works as a freelance photographer based in Shipley, England.

© 1998 Gary Freeman

In the small town of Moravia, Czech Republic, a blind woman cares for her elderly and frail husband. While he takes a rest, she reads to him from a book written in Braille.

Canon EOS 1N, 28 mm, Kodak Tri-X/135, Exp. f5.6-1/125

David Sanchez Gimenez
SPAIN

David Sanchez Gimenez was born in Terrassa, Spain. He discovered photography while travelling around the world and went on to study at the Grisart School of Photography in Barcelona. David has been a full-time professional photographer since 1998. His images have been published in numerous newspapers and magazines and have won three awards in Spanish photographic competitions.

© 1999 David Sanchez Gimenez

A cheeky young couple distract Alfonso from his newspaper as he waits for his bus in Barcelona, Spain.

Leica M6, 2.8/28 mm, Kodak Tri-X/135, Exp. N/A

Lynn Goldsmith
USA

Lynn Goldsmith is a self-taught photographer based in New York, USA, and known for her celebrity portraiture. She has won many prizes for her work, including the World Press, Lucien Clerque and NCP International awards. Lynn's photographs have appeared in numerous international publications such as *Time*, *Life*, *Sports Illustrated* and *Rolling Stone*. She has held a solo exhibition at the International Center of Photography, New York, and published seven books of her work.

© 1986 Lynn Goldsmith

A little girl holds tightly to her grandmother's hand as they walk together in Arles, France.

Nikon F, 108 mm, Ektachrome 100/135, Exp. 5.6-1/250

Ário Gonçalves
BRAZIL

Ário Gonçalves was born in Porto Alegre, Brazil, and his first experience of photography was selling photographic equipment. In 1992 he decided to further his interest and was accepted in the 19th Youth Photo Forum of FIAP, the International Federation of Photographic Art. Currently Ário works as a photographer for the Criminal Department of Brazil.

© 1999 Ário Gonçalves

In Alvorado, Brazil, a gentle kiss from her mother, Rosângela, elicits a happy gurgle from three-month-old Ariane.

Olympus OM20, 35–105 mm, Kodak Tri-X 400/135, Exp. f3.5-1/30

Dylan Griffin
USA

Dylan Griffin studied at the Saint Edwards University in Austin, Texas, USA. He was awarded the Santa Fe Photographic Workshop scholarship and the Ruth Long scholarship based on his work there. He now lives and works in New York.

© 1998 Dylan Griffin

Photographer Dylan Griffin captured this image of his girlfriend's uncles at a hot spring resort near Las Cruces, New Mexico, USA. David and Jeff share a beer, and a dress code, as they relax together.

Rollei 6006, 50 mm, Kodak Tri-X/120, Exp. f8-1/60

Michael Hagedorn
GERMANY

Michael Hagedorn is a freelance photojournalist based in Rellingen near Hamburg, Germany. He works on German and international magazines and newspapers as well as in the corporate sector. Currently Michael is working on a long-term photographic project about the island of Java, as well as collecting material for a new book, *Age and Death*.

© 1999 Michael Hagedorn

Late love – Walter surprises Frieda with a spontaneous kiss as they walk through the park in Henningsdorf, Germany. Although Walter and Frieda had known each other a long time, it was only when they were both widowed and living as neighbours in a retirement home that their love blossomed.

Canon EOS 5, 45 mm, Kodak T400 CN/135, Exp. N/A

Patrick Hamilton
AUSTRALIA

Patrick Hamilton has worked as a professional photojournalist for 13 years. Currently he lives in Brisbane, Australia, and works for the *Australian* newspaper. Patrick has won numerous awards at home and abroad, including the 1998 Walkley Award for excellence in journalism.

© 1989 Patrick Hamilton

Still in love after 65 years of marriage – Theo kisses his wife goodbye as he leaves for another day at his workshop. The couple, both 85 years old, were photographed in their home in Toowoomba, in Queensland, Australia.

Nikon F3, 35 mm, Kodak T-max 400/135, Exp. f2.8-1/60

David Hancock
AUSTRALIA

David Hancock was born in New Zealand and his varied career includes time spent as a labourer and a stonemason. He has worked as a freelance photographer on newspapers and magazines for over 20 years and today lives in Sydney, Australia.

© 1992 David Hancock

Arm in arm – sharing sunshine and shopping on a day trip to Manly, a seaside suburb of Sydney, Australia.

Bronica ETRS, 50 mm, Kodak T-max/120, Exp. f8-1/125

Mark Edward Harris
USA

Mark Edward Harris graduated with a Master of Arts degree from California State University, USA, and is now a photographer, writer and teacher based in Los Angeles. He has won many awards. His work has appeared in publications including *Time*, *Life*, *Vogue* and *People*. His book *Faces of the Twentieth Century: Master Photographers and Their Work* won Photography Book of the Year at the New York Book Show in 1999.

© 1997 Mark Edward Harris

A dog gives his young owner an affectionate lick during their impromptu waltz. The photographer captured this image of his eight-year-old nephew and friend at their home in Boston, Massachusetts, USA.

Nikon N90S, 35 mm, Kodak T-max 3200/135, Exp. f2.8-1/125

Linda Heim
USA

Linda Heim lives in Delmar in Albany, in the state of New York, and was trained as a physical education teacher. She is a serious amateur photographer and enjoys capturing a range of subject matter on film.

© 1999 Linda Heim

Lynn and her 10-month-old son, Casey, try a new variation of rock-a-bye-baby on the shore of Burden Lake in New York state, USA.

Canon T90, 28–200 mm, Kodak/135, Exp. N/A

Henry Hill
USA

Henry Hill's interest in photography began in the 1960s when he joined a photo club while in the Navy. He became a photographer and is currently based in Florissant, Colorado. Henry concentrates mainly on fashion portfolio, portraiture and wedding work, and his images have appeared in travel publications, newspapers and speciality magazines.

© 1999 Henry Hill

Eight-day-old Cyrus is content and secure as he lies sleepily on his father Joe. The young baby had only just left hospital and this image was taken on his first day at home in Colorado Springs, Colorado, USA.

Pentax 67(2), 105 mm, Kodak/120, Exp. f5.6-1/30

Sándor Horváth
ROMANIA

Sándor Horváth is based in the Romanian town of TG-Mures. He graduated in mathematics from the University of Bucharest and now works as a lecturer at two different universities in Romania. His interest in photography began just one year ago.

© 1999 Sándor Horváth

The long road – an elderly man sees that his young relative comes to no harm as they make their way towards a small town in Transylvania, Romania.

Minolta Dynax 500SI, Sigma 100–300 mm, Fuji Superia 200/135, Exp. 1/250

Zhiyao Jiang
AUSTRALIA

Zhiyao Jiang studied English language and literature at Shanghai Normal University in China and worked as a teacher after graduation. He is a keen amateur photographer and in 1985 became the winner of the grand final of the Shanghai black and white photographic competition. Zhiyao moved to Australia in 1986 and the following year won first prize in the Royal Melbourne Institute for Technology photographic contest.

© 1999 Zhiyao Jiang

On a hot day in Melbourne, Australia, two friends share a refreshing drink at a water fountain. As the dog looks on, a young couple hold each other close.

Contax T2, Sonnar 38 mm, Kodak T-max 400/135, Exp. f5.6-1/125

Lorenz Kienzle
GERMANY

Lorenz Kienzle was born in Germany and began his career working as a fashion photographer's assistant. He undertook formal training at the Lette Verein photography school in Berlin and has worked as a freelance photographer since 1993.

© 1999 Lorenz Kienzle

A family lies in relaxed contentment on the shore of the River Elbe in Germany. While his parents sleep off their picnic lunch, three-month-old Jan enjoys a drink of his own.

Nikon FM2, 35 mm, Agfa 100/135, Exp. f5.6-1/60

Jarek Kret
POLAND

Jarek Kret studied Egyptology at Warsaw University in Poland. After graduation, he worked for Polish national television and, over a three-year period, made 150 television shows and 20 TV documentaries. Jarek has written two books and now works on the editorial staff of the Polish edition of *National Geographic* magazine.

© 1996 Jarek Kret

In a remote village on the west coast of Madagascar, a young woman is oblivious to the photographer's presence as he captures this tender image of her watching over her young child.

Canon EOS Elan IIe, 75–300 mm, Fuji/135, Exp. N/A

Tzer Luck Lau
SINGAPORE

Tzer Luck Lau has been interested in photography since 1986. After achieving a diploma in graphic design, he has worked as a photo assistant, digital imaging artist and a graphic designer while pursuing a personal interest in photography. He lives and works in Singapore.

© 1998 Tzer Luck Lau

Intimacy does not require privacy when you're a teenager living in Manhattan. These young students are absorbed in their own passionate world on a busy street in New York, USA.

Leica R6, 35 mm, Kodak Tri-X/135, Exp. N/A

Al Lieberman
USA

Al Lieberman grew up in Chicago, Illinois, and had an early interest in art. He graduated with a Master of Arts Education degree from the School of the Art Institute in Chicago and is currently an elementary school art educator. Al's interest in photography began in the 1960s when he photographed the Democratic Convention in Chicago. Today his photographs appear in the permanent collections of the Museum of Modern Art in New York, and the American Museum of the Smithsonian in Washington DC, USA.

© Al Lieberman [date N/A]

The usual routine – side by side, an elderly couple patiently wait for their washing to dry. They are residents of Sun City Arizona, a retirement community in the USA.

Leica M3, 50 mm, Kodak Tri-X/135, Exp. f5.6-1/125

Robert Lifson
USA

Robert Lifson has been a photographer for over 20 years. He has travelled throughout Europe, Mexico and the USA with his work and has received numerous awards. His images have been exhibited in galleries and museums worldwide, and appear in public and private collections. Robert currently works as a staff photographer at the Art Institute of Chicago, Illinois.

© Robert Lifson [date N/A]

On a pedestal – a farmer looks up to his wife in the rural village of Ruseni, Romania.

Rolleiflex TLR, 75 mm, Ilford FP4/120, Exp. f3.5-1/50

Kelley Loveridge
NEW ZEALAND

Kelley Loveridge was born in New Zealand and, at the age of 17, began a photo-journalism cadetship. She left her home country to work abroad, and spent a year working as a portrait photographer in London, England. Kelley returned to New Zealand to pursue her career as a professional photographer and recently set up her own company in Auckland, etc. Photography and Design.

© 1999 Kelley Loveridge

An intimate moment for this expectant couple in Auckland, New Zealand.

Nikon F90X, 2.8/80–200 mm, Kodak Tri-X/135, Exp. N/A

Madan Mahatta
INDIA

Madan Mahatta was born in Kashmir, India, and graduated from the Guildford School of Arts and Crafts in Surrey, England. He is now one of the managing directors of a photographic company in New Delhi, India. Madan has won numerous national and international awards and has been a judge for photographic competitions in India.

© 1975 Madan Mahatta

While his parents visit a camel fair in the desert of Rajasthan, India, a young child enjoys the tender love and care of his grandfather.

Nikon F2, 135 mm, Kodak Tri-X/135, Exp. f2.8-1/500

Karen Maini
USA

Karen Maini has been a keen photographer since an early age. Currently she is based in New York.

© 1997 Karen Maini

A peaceful moment at the Zen Mountain Monastery on Mount Tremper, in the state of New York, USA.

Rolleiflex, 3.5/75 mm, Kodak Tri-X/120, Exp. f8-1/125

Piotr Malecki
POLAND

Piotr Malecki was born in Poland and studied film-making in the city of Katowice. He travelled to England to study art and photography at the Bournemouth and Poole College of Art and Design. After returning to Poland, he became a professional photographer and is currently based in Warsaw.

© 1994 Piotr Malecki

A train station in Tallinn, Estonia, is the setting for tearful farewells as sailors from the Russian fleet say goodbye to their Estonian girlfriends.

Konica Hexar, 35 mm, Ilford HP5/135, Exp. N/A

Marcio RM
BRAZIL

Marcio Resende De Mendonca E Silva has worked as a professional photographer in Brazil since 1982, under the professional name of Marcio RM.Since then his photographs have appeared in a variety of Brazilian publications including *Isto É* magazine and the *O Estado de São Paolo* newspaper. Marcio has also participated in exhibitions in Brazil and abroad.

© 1991 Marcio RM

As the parade passes by in the Rio de Janeiro carnival, Brazil, a young couple share an affectionate kiss amid the crowd.

Canon F1, 85 mm, Ilford HP5 Plus/135, Exp. f2.8-1/1000

Tatiana D Matthews
SPAIN

Tatiana D Matthews was born in Chile. She studied for a history of art degree at the University of Barcelona in Spain and began her professional photography career in 1998.

© 1998 Tatiana D Matthews

Merce, 32, is about to give birth to her third child at home in Argentona, Spain. Her first two children were born in hospital, but this time she has chosen to have her baby at home, in the company of family and friends. Her partner, Enric, massages her back to ease the pain of labour.

Nikon FM, 35 mm, Kodak T-max/135, Exp. N/A

John McNamara
USA

John McNamara graduated with a Master of Arts from the University of San Francisco in California. Today he is an independent photojournalist. John's images have won national and international awards and he was an Honourable Mention winner in the Best of Photography 1999 contest. He donates his professional time as the publicity photographer for the Special Olympics.

© 1999 John McNamara

The Special Olympics in Union City, California – father Daryl gives his son, JR, a hug full of love and pride after the young competitor finishes his event.

Canon EOS 1, 2.8/300 mm, Ilford HP5 Plus/135, Exp. 1/1000

Melissa Mermin
USA

Melissa Mermin graduated in painting from the Massachusetts College of Art, USA, and then went on to study photojournalism. Today she lives in Cambridge, Massachusetts, where she works as a photographer.

© 1998 Melissa Mermin

Wedding preparations in Boston, USA – against all tradition, the groom, Doug, sneaks a kiss from his bride, Jennifer, before they get dressed for the occasion.

Canon A2, 24 mm, Ilford XP2/135, Exp. f5.6-1/30

Stacey P Morgan
USA

Stacey P Morgan has been a professional photojournalist for over 15 years. She has been a contract photographer for the *New York Times*, the *Baltimore Sun* and the *Philadelphia Inquirer*. Her work has also appeared in magazines including *Sports Illustrated*, *Golf Illustrated* and *Vogue*. Stacey has won over 40 awards in national and international competitions, and has exhibited work in galleries, museums and collections around the world.

© 1992 Stacey P Morgan

In New York, Anne and her young son Robert discover that the bedroom is the perfect place for hide and seek.

Nikon, 2.8/20 mm, Kodak Tri-X 400/135, Exp. N/A

Debashis Mukherjee (Deba)
INDIA

Deba (Debashis Mukherjee) is a science graduate and works in banking in Calcutta, India. His serious interest in photography began in 1996 and he is now studying for a diploma in the subject.

© 1999 Debashis Mukherjee

In the village of Champahati, India, a 70-year-old grandmother enjoys a restful break after a meal. Her young grandson gently holds her hands as they share this special time together.

Pentax K1000, 28 mm, Ilford/135, Exp. f2.8-1/8

Y Nagasaki
USA

Y Nagasaki was born in Japan and now lives in New York, USA. He is a graduate of the Aoyama Gakuin University in Tokyo and the Long Island University in New York. He also received a Master of Fine Arts degree in photography from New York's City University. Y Nagasaki works as a professional photographer and has been exhibited and published internationally.

© 1989 Y Nagasaki

Holding hands in the surf – an elderly couple get away from it all on Sandy Hook beach in New Jersey, USA.

Nikon F4S, Nikkor 35–70 mm, Kodak Tri-X/135, Exp. N/A

WINNER OF THE "LOVE" CATEGORY IN THE M.I.L.K. PHOTOGRAPHIC COMPETITION.

Abel Naim
VENEZUELA

Abel Naim studied film and photography in Valencia, Venezuela. After graduation, he became a freelance editorial photographer and his work has been published in leading art and photography magazines in his home country. Abel's images have also appeared in exhibitions in Brazil, Canada, Cuba, Finland and the USA.

© 1993 Abel Naim

During a workshop for the underprivileged communities of Caracas, Venezuela, children learn how to communicate with others and to express their emotions. As the instructor, Durbin, gives her young student a hug, their faces light up with love and happiness.

Canon AE1, 135 mm, Kodak/135, Exp. f2.5-1/60

J D Nielsen
USA

J D Nielsen was born in California, USA, and served for 21 years in the US Navy. During this time, he travelled extensively in the USA, Europe, Asia and Central America. He is now studying photojournalism and hopes to follow a career in photography.

© 1999 J D Nielsen

Joe's special relationship with his wife is obvious to visitors to his shoe repair shop in Covina, California, USA.

Nikon F2, 55 mm, Kodak T-max 400/135, Exp. N/A

Ricardo Ordóñez
CANADA

Ricardo Ordóñez was born in Ottawa, Canada, but has lived in various countries in the Caribbean and South America, as well as the USA and Canada. A self-taught photographer, he has worked for over 13 years for a wide variety of clients and across a broad subject range. His business operates under the name of PhotoSure.com. His work as a photographer has been profiled in the international media.

© 1990 Ricardo Ordóñez/PhotoSure.com

The 60th wedding anniversary – love, respect and six decades of marriage bind husband and wife Henri and Violet Mayoux. They exchange a humorous look as they prepare to cut their anniversary cake in Ontario, Canada.

Nikon F4S, 2.8/35–70 mm, Kodak Ektachrome/135, Exp. f4-1/60

Jacqueline Parker
UK

Jacqueline Parker is a graduate in editorial photography. Currently she is studying for a Master of Arts degree in illustration and sequential design at Brighton University in England.

© 1999 Jacqueline Parker

The best of friends – inseparable childhood companions Christopher, aged seven, and his dog Billy take a break from making mischief.

Bronica SQA, 80 mm, Kodak T-max/120, Exp. f11-1/250

George Peirce
USA

George Peirce graduated in photography from the State University of New York in New Paltz, USA. He began his freelance photography career in 1984 and now works as a commercial photographer specializing in architectural and industrial photography. His work is published in journals, magazines, books and advertisements. George also undertakes fine art photography and his images have been exhibited across the USA.

© 1998 George Peirce

Puppy love in Point Pleasant, New Jersey, USA. Twelve-year-old DD and her sister Georgia, 10, are delighted with their new pet. Their photographer father, George Peirce, captured this moment as they met eight-week-old Atlantis for the very first time.

Leica CL, Summicron-C 40 mm, Kodak T-max 400/135, Exp. f4-1/125

Renate Pfleiderer
USA

Renate Pfleiderer studied in Germany for a Masters degree in photography. She worked as a fashion and advertising photographer in her own studio in Hamburg, Germany, before moving to the USA. Today Renate has a studio, Photo Renate, in Sag Harbor, New York state, and specializes in portrait, wedding and art photography. She has won many awards during her career and her work has been featured in several magazines and on television.

© 1998 Renate Pfleiderer

Newly wedded bliss on Long Island, New York – Travis catches Camille's wedding veil when it blows off in the wind, but he can't resist trying it on before returning it to his new wife.

Leica R4, 35–70 mm, Kodak TMZ/135, Exp. f16-1/250

Kamthorn Pongsutiyakorn
THAILAND

Kamthorn Pongsutiyakorn is a photography and film graduate from Thailand's Bangkok Technical Campus. He now runs his own photo studio in the Chonburi region of Thailand.

© 1998 Kamthorn Pongsutiyakorn

A grandmother with her granddaughter in the backyard of their home in Chonburi, Thailand.

Contax 167MT, 80–200 mm, Agfa/135,Exp. f4-1/60

Romualdas Požerskis
LITHUANIA

Romualdas Požerskis studied electrical engineering at Kaunas Polytechnic Institute, Lithuania, and went on to work at the Photography Art Society of Lithuania. He has been a freelance photographer since 1980 and is a university lecturer in the history and aesthetics of photography. Romualdas was the 1991 winner of the Lithuanian National Award for cultural achievement and, in 1994, he became an artist of FIAP, the International Federation of Photographic Art.

© 1987 Romualdas Požerskis

A secret meal – in Lithuania, an elderly woman continues to feed her beloved cats even though it is forbidden by her landlords.

Minolta X700, 70–210 mm, Svema 400/136, Exp. f5.6-1/250

© 1978 Romualdas Požerskis

In a small town in Lithuania, families come together once a year for their own Catholic pilgrimage. After a day of celebration, two elderly relatives bid each other farewell before heading home.

Minolta SRT102, 50 mm, Svema 400/136, Exp. f11-1/250

Devang Prajapati
INDIA

Devang Prajapati comes from a family of visual artists – his father and grandfather are portrait artists and his uncle is a commercial photographer. Devang worked as an art teacher for five years before becoming a freelance photographer. He is based in Ahmedabad, India.

© 1999 Devang Prajapati

In the town of Ahmedabad, India, one-year-old Forum is fascinated by the face of elderly neighbour Mrs Champaben.

Nikon FM10, 35–70 mm, Fuji/135, Exp. f8-1/60

Jeremy Rall
USA

Through his background in editorial and still photography, Jeremy Rall developed an interest in film-making and went on to study film production at the University of Notre Dame, USA. After graduating, he received the James O'Toole Award for achievement in film production and was selected to participate in a fellowship programme at the American Film Institute. Jeremy is now a director, editor and photographer based in Los Angeles, California.

© 1998 Jeremy Rall

A father lifts up his young son to give him a better view of a street festival in Santa Monica, California, USA.

Pentax Super ME, 50 mm, Kodak Plus-X 125/125, Exp. N/A

Sayyed Nayyer Reza
PAKISTAN

Sayyed Nayyer Reza is based in Lahore, Pakistan. His images have been exhibited in 35 countries around the world and have won him numerous awards. Sayyed has been ranked among the top 25 exhibitors of the world for colour print photography by the Photographic Society of America for the last six years. He is also an artist of FIAP, the International Federation of Photographic Art.

© 1993 Sayyed Nayyer Reza

Love and kindness bridge the generation gap in Lahore, Pakistan. Nine-year-old Suman shares a playful moment with her elderly friend and neighbour – the old lady is known simply as Amman, an Urdu word for "mother".

Nikon F45, 35–105 mm, Fuji Reala/135, Exp. f5.6-1/60

Marc Rochette
CANADA

Marc Rochette has been a photographer for 20 years and his work includes editorial, documentary, wedding and commercial photography. Based in Canada, he began his career as a freelancer and then worked as a staff photographer for a weekly newspaper. Marc is now a full-time freelance photographer working in Toronto.

© 1999 Marc Rochette

A look of love and encouragement from father to daughter. Six-year-old Erica's soccer team from Bramalea, Canada, may not win very often, but her father is always on hand to support her efforts in the game.

Nikon F90X, 2.8/80–200 mm, Kodak T-max 400/135, Exp. f5.6

Lydia Linda Ruscitto
ITALY

Lydia Linda Ruscitto was born in New York, USA, and now lives in Anguillara Sabazia, Italy. She is a graduate in German literature, but also has a strong interest in geology and biology. She has used these scientific themes in her photographic work, contributing many images to the Italian photographic agency Homoambiens.

© 1998 Lydia Linda Ruscitto

Nose to nose – as brother and sister Alessandro and Martina act up for the camera in Trento, Italy.

Nikon F801, 90 mm, Fuji/135, Exp. f8

Ivo Saglietti
ITALY

Ivo Saglietti is based in Milan, Italy. He has been a photographic journalist since 1978 and has worked on news reports in Latin America, Africa and the Middle East for various Italian and international newspapers.

© 1997 Ivo Saglietti

Gentle touch – a Cuban doctor gives a young Chernobyl victim a compassionate kiss. Children from the Chernobyl region in the Ukraine have been receiving hospital treatment in Cuba since the nuclear disaster.

Canon Reflex F1, 24 mm, Kodak Tri-X/135, Exp. f2-1/15

Gundula Schulze-Eldowy
GERMANY

Gundula Schulze-Eldowy was born in East Germany and studied photography at the School for Graphic and Book Art in Leipzig. She has been a freelance photographer since 1985 and has lived in Germany, Egypt and the USA. Gundula's work has appeared in exhibitions in Europe, Asia and America. Her images have also been sold to the Museum of Modern Art in New York and the Bibliothèque Nationale in Paris, France.

© 1987 Gundula Schulze-Eldowy

Photographer Gundula Schulze-Eldowy can't help laughing as her friend Stephen tickles her. She set the camera on automatic to capture this spontaneous self-portrait in a local park near her home in the Pankow district of Berlin, Germany.

Nikon FE, 50 mm, Orwo-NP 20/135, Exp. N/A

Josef Sekal
CZECH REPUBLIC

Josef Sekal lives in Prague, Czech Republic, and has been a keen photographer for nearly 50 years. He became a professional freelancer in 1970 after winning the International Phototechnik Competition in Munich, Germany. Since then his architecture and landscape images have appeared in books, calendars and postcards. Now retired, Josef continues to travel the world in search of photo opportunities.

© 1974 Josef Sekal

Outdoor pursuit – a park bench makes a change from the sofa for an elderly couple winding a ball of wool in Prague, Czech Republic.

Linhof Super Technika IV, 95 mm, Agfachrome/4"x5", Exp. f8-1/30

Ricardo Serpa
BRAZIL

Ricardo Serpa worked as an export executive travelling around Latin America before his interest turned to photography. He left his job to join a newspaper in Rio de Janeiro, Brazil, and now works as a freelance photographer in that city.

© 1989 Ricardo Serpa

While the traffic rumbles by on the streets of Rio de Janeiro, Brazil, a homeless man sleeps serenely with some support from a friend.

Nikon FM2, 85 mm, Kodak Tri-X/135, Exp. N/A

Yew Fatt Siew
MALAYSIA

Yew Fatt Siew is based in Kuala Lumpur, Malaysia, and has been a keen photographer since he was at school. He is now a semi-retired businessman and works in housing development throughout Asia. His work in China brings opportunities to photograph the country's people and places in his spare time.

© 1994 Yew Fatt Siew

A Buddhist festival at Labuleng Lamasery in Gansu, China – in sub-zero temperatures, a Tibetan mother's embrace offers protection and warmth.

Nikon F4S, 4.5/70–300 mm, Fuji RVP/135, Exp. f8-1/125

John Siu
AUSTRALIA

John Siu is a photographer with over 40 years' experience. He is based in Killara, in New South Wales, Australia, where he specializes in personal and group souvenir photographs for tourists. John is President of the Chinese Photographic Society of Australia and a member of the Australian Photographic Society in Hong Kong.

© 1998 John Siu

On a street in North Vietnam, the happy exuberance of a young child and the warm, patient smile of her grandmother convey a loving relationship across the generations.

Leica R8, 28–70 mm, Fuji/135, Exp. 1/200

Steven G Smith
USA

Steven G Smith has been a professional photographer for over 15 years. He has worked on various newspapers throughout the USA and is currently based in New Mexico.

© 1992 Steven G Smith

Sharing a smile – old friends Nellie and Violet are in playful mood at their nursing home in Ohio, USA.

Canon EOS 1, 24 mm, Kodak/135, Exp. f4-1/60

Evžen Sobek
CZECH REPUBLIC

Evžen Sobek studied for a Masters qualification in medical engineering in Brno, Czech Republic. He went on to gain a Master of Arts degree from the Institute of Creative Photography in the city of Opava. Since 1995, he has worked as a freelance photographer and teacher in Brno.

© 1998 Evžen Sobek

A lazy Sunday for members of the Gypsy community of Brno, Czech Republic – Tibor and Tomáš catch up on sleep and the weekend newspaper.

Canon F1, 28 mm, Foma/135, Exp. f4-1/15

Tino Soriano
SPAIN

Tino Soriano is a freelance photographer based in Barcelona, Spain. His images have been published in magazines throughout the world including *Paris Match*, *Der Spiegel* and *National Geographic*. Tino has won numerous awards, including the Spanish Fotopres award for the best press photograph of the year on five separate occasions. In 1999, he won first prize in the "Art" category of the World Press Photo contest.

© 1999 Tino Soriano

Rain delays the beginning of a carnival in Barahona, Dominican Republic. A young couple exchange a flirtatious glance as they wait for the festivities to begin.

Leica M6, 2.8/35 mm, Kodak T-max 400/135, Exp. f5.6-1/250

Harvey Stein
USA

Harvey Stein's photographs have appeared in over 50 solo exhibitions and 90 group shows in the USA and Europe, and can be found in more than 35 public and private collections. Currently he teaches photography at Drew University in New Jersey, and the International Center of Photography and the New School for Social Research in New York, USA. Harvey has had three books of photographs published and his work has appeared in publications including *Time*, *Life*, the *New York Times* and *Der Spiegel*.

© 1998 Harvey Stein

In their own world – an amorous pair share hugs and kisses on a doorstep in Florence, Italy, oblivious to the passers-by.

Leica M4, 21 mm, Kodak Plus-X/135, Exp. f8-1/125

Milo Stewart Jr
USA

Milo Stewart Jr is a second-generation professional photographer based in New York. He was a competent photographer by the age of 10 and his work has appeared in several local galleries. Currently Milo works as the chief photographer for the National Baseball Hall of Fame and Museum in Cooperstown, New York.

© 1999 Milo Stewart Jr

In Cooperstown, New York, new mother Leslie is enchanted with her baby son Bartow.

Rolleiflex TLR, 75 mm, Kodak Tri-X/135, Exp. f5.6-1/15

Maňo Štrauch
SLOVAK REPUBLIC

Maňo Štrauch was born in Slovakia. After studying economics at university, he began work as a freelance photographer and has spent time working in the USA, as well as in Slovakia. Today he is based in Bratislava in the Slovak Republic and works for newspapers, magazines and a number of charitable organizations. Maňo won the Czech Press Photo award in 1998 and 1999.

© 1997 Maňo Štrauch

Outside a Franciscan church in the Slovak Republic, a homeless couple steal a kiss. They are hoping for charitable gifts from the departing congregation. Their three-month-old son, Ivanko, born in an underground cave on the outskirts of the city, yawns as he waits.

Nikon FM2, Nikkor 60 mm, Ilford Pan 400/135, Exp. f8-1/125

Jindřich Štreit
CZECH REPUBLIC

Jindřich Štreit was born in Vsetín, Czech Republic, and studied art education at Palacký University in the city of Olomouc. In 1982, he participated in an unofficial exhibition of alternative art which led to his arrest by the secret police and the confiscation of his photographic equipment. He was not able to pursue his interest in photography until after the Velvet Revolution of 1989. Today Jindřich works as a freelance photographer based in Brno, Czech Republic. He also teaches photography at the FAMU Film Academy in Prague and the Silesian University in Opava.

© 1997 Jindřich Štreit

Boy meets girl – in the small village of Kižinga in Southern Siberia, Russia.

Nikon FM2, 28 mm, Kodak T-max 400/135, Exp. f5.6-1/125

Venkata Sunder Rao Pampana (Sunder)
INDIA

Sunder was born in Guntur in Andhra Pradesh, India. He began his photography career as a laboratory technician and now runs his own custom colour studio in Vijayawada, India. He has been a keen competitive photographer since 1988 and has won prizes in a number of national contests.

© 1998 Venkata Sunder Rao Pampana

A tender touch – a young girl looks after her baby sister asleep in a hammock made from her mother's sari. Without a permanent home, the family lives on the streets of Vijayawada in India.

Nikon Nikkormat, Nikor 1.4/50 mm, Kodak Gold/135, Exp. f5.6-1/125

Sam Tanner
UK

Sam Tanner worked as a sculptor before he decided to become a full-time professional photographer 12 years ago. He concentrates particularly on documentary work in the UK, including aspects of the National Health Service, the work of carers, and life in the Jewish community of East London. In 1999 Sam won first prize in the professional category of the *Independent on Sunday* photography competition.

© 1999 Sam Tanner

Laughter and a loving embrace for a Jewish couple celebrating 61 years of marriage. Dave, 89, and his wife Renee, 82, live in the East End of London, England.

Leica M6, 35 mm, Kodak/135, Exp. f5.6-1/30

Sam Devine Tischler
USA

Sam Devine Tischler grew up in Santa Fe, New Mexico, and moved to Seattle to study commercial photography at the Seattle Art Institute. After graduation, he moved back to his home town where he has pursued a career in professional photography.

© 1997 Sam Devine Tischler

The photographer captured this affectionate image of his grandfather Max, 86, and grandmother Ann, 80, in New Port Richie, Florida, USA.

Nikon F3, 100 mm, Kodak/135, Exp. f8-1/125

Peter Van Hoof
BELGIUM

Peter Van Hoof studied film and photography at the Royal Academy of Fine Arts in Ghent, Belgium. After graduation, he worked as a darkroom assistant and photo editor for a newspaper before becoming a freelance photographer. Currently Peter lives in Ghent and works for magazines in Belgium and the Netherlands.

© 1996 Peter Van Hoof

Love and tenderness in a sleepy embrace for two young children on Chiloe Island, Chile.

Nikon FM2, Kodak T-max 400/135, Exp. N/A

Wilfred Van Zyl
SOUTH AFRICA

Wilfred Van Zyl studied photography at the Port Elizabeth Technikon in South Africa. After graduation he worked as a professional photographer for six years. Today Wilfred runs his own photographic business in East London, South Africa.

© 1998 Wilfred Van Zyl

Six-year-old Marcelle holds on tight as her father, the photographer, takes her for a spin. To achieve the effect, Wilfred Van Zyl strapped the camera to his chest and used the self-timer to capture his daughter's delighted smile as he swings her through the air. The reflection of the photographer can be seen in the little girl's eyes.

Canon T90, 2.8/24 mm, Agfapan APX 100/135, Exp. f11-1/30

Frank White
USA

Frank White is a professional photographer and educator based in Houston, Texas. He graduated from the Rochester Institute of Technology in New York in 1977 and set up his own commercial photography studio the following year. Since 1982, he has taught photography at the School of Architecture at Rice University, Houston.

© 1989 Frank White

In Houston, Texas, USA, Jo-Anne cuddles her five-year-old daughter, Ellen, in a loving and protective embrace. They are smiling at the photographer – husband and father Frank White.

Hasselblad ELX, 150 mm, Kodak T-max 100/120, Exp. N/A

Desmond Williams
NEW ZEALAND

Desmond Williams is a New Zealander who has worked in studios in England, Australia and Germany as well as in his home country. Currently he works as a diving instructor and underwater photographer on boats cruising Papua New Guinea and the Great Barrier Reef, Australia.

© 1998 Desmond Williams

The isolated island of Darnley in the Torres Strait between Australia and Papua New Guinea – Father Pilot, the village priest, outside his church.

Hasselblad ELX, Zeiss 40 mm, Kodak E100SW/120, Exp. f16-1/125

Jia Lin Wu
CHINA

Jia Lin Wu was born in Yunnan province, China. He graduated from the Affiliated Middle School of Yunnan University in 1961 and began working in photography eight years later. Since then, his work has appeared in several exhibitions and books. In 1997 he received the *Mother Jones* Documentary Photographic Award.

© 1982 Jia Lin Wu

The family bond begins at an early age for a young brother and sister in Lancang, China.

China Haiou, 58 mm, Fuji 100/135, Exp. N/A

Jane Wyles
NEW ZEALAND

Jane Wyles studied photography at Christchurch Polytechnic, New Zealand. During her course, she specialized in black and white images and particularly those documenting human relationships. She now works as a freelance photographer based in Christchurch.

© 1999 Jane Wyles

Laughter is infectious for father and son, Drew and James, as they share an affectionate hug in Christchurch, New Zealand.

Nikon F90X, 50 mm, Kodak T400 CN/135, Exp. f5.6-1/125

Nigel Yates
NEW ZEALAND

Nigel Yates was born in Bradford, England, and emigrated with his family to New Zealand. His photography career began in 1976 when he worked for the *Otago Daily Times* in New Zealand. Nigel went on to work with a number of different newspapers as well as magazines and theatres. He has also published a photography book depicting life in Dunedin, New Zealand.

© 1995 Nigel Yates

A shy smile from an old romantic as he and his two companions look forward to a rendezvous outside a jewellery shop in Dublin, Ireland.

Leica M2, 2/35 mm, Kodak Tri-X/135, Exp. f8-1/125

Simon Young
NEW ZEALAND

Simon Young is a photography graduate from the Elam School of Fine Arts in New Zealand. Currently he is based in Auckland and works as a freelance photographer specializing in editorial work for magazines.

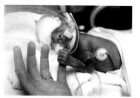

© 1999 Simon Young

At a hospital in Auckland, New Zealand, a baby boy's tiny hand grips his mother's finger. This is the very first bonding between the mother and her four-day-old son after his premature birth.

Nikon F90, 55 mm, Kodak T400 CN/135, Exp. N/A

MOMENTS INTIMACY LAUGHTER KINSHIP

First published in Great Britain in 2002 by HEADLINE BOOK PUBLISHING. A division of Hodder Headline, 338 Euston Road, London, NW1 3BH.

The following individuals, companies, and organizations were significant contributors to the development of M.I.L.K. – Ruth Hamilton, Ruth-Anna Hobday, Claudia Hood, Nicola Henderson, Liz McRae, Brian Ross, Don Neely, Kai Brethouwer, Vicki Smith, Rebecca Swan, Bound to Last, Designworks, Image Centre Limited, Logan Brewer Production Design Limited, KPMG Legal, Lowe Lintas & Partners, Midas Printing Group Limited, MTA Arts for Transit, Print Management Consultants, Sauvage Design, Mary-Ann Lewis, Vibeke Brethouwer and Karen Pearson.

Special thanks also to David Baldock, Julika Batten, Anne Bayin, Sue Bidwill, Janet Blackwell, John Blackwell, Susanna Blackwell, Sandra Bloodworth, Sonia Carroll, Mona Chen, Patrick Cox, Malcolm Edwards, Michael Fleck, Lisa Highton, Anne Hoy, C K Lau, Liz Meyers, James Mora, Paddianne Neely, Grant Nola, Ricardo Ordóñez, Kim Phuc, Chris Pitt, Tanya Robertson, Margaret Sinclair, Marlis Teubner, Nicki White.

The publisher is grateful for permission to reproduce those items below subject to copyright. While every effort has been made to trace copyright holders, the publisher would be pleased to hear from any not acknowledged here.

Competition Chief Judge Elliott Erwitt. Designed by Lucy Richardson. Printed by Midas Printing Limited, Hong Kong.

British Library Cataloguing in Publication Data for this title is available on request.

ISBN 0 7553 1161 2